LIFE CYCLES

Chicken

Ruth Thomson

WAYLAND

Explore the world with **Popcorn** - your complete first non-fiction library.

Look out for more titles in the **Popcorn** range. All books have the same format of simple text and awesome images. Text is carefully matched to the pictures to help readers to identify and understand key vocabulary.
www.waylandbooks.co.uk/popcorn

First published in 2009 by Wayland

Copyright © Wayland 2009

Wayland
Hachette Children's Books
338 Euston Road
London NW1 3BH

Wayland Australia
Level 17/207 Kent Street
Sydney NSW 2000

Managing Editor: Victoria Brooker
Concept designer: Paul Cherrill

British Library Cataloguing in Publication Data:
Thomson, Ruth
  Chicken. - (Popcorn: Life Cycles)
  1. Chickens - Life cycles - Juvenile literature
  I Title
  571.8'18625

ISBN: 978 0 7502 5784 8

Printed and bound in China

Wayland is a division of Hachette Children's Books,
an Hachette UK Company.

www.hachettelivre.co.uk

Photographs:
Cover, title page, 4/5, 6, 7, 8, 10, 18, 20 Photolibrary Group; 9 Robert Pickett/Papilio; 10, 12, 13 Ernie Janes/NHPA/Photoshot; 11, 14 © DK Limited/CORBIS; 15 © Herbert Spichtinger/zefa/Corbis; 16 Jane Burton/DK/Getty Images; 17 © DK Limited/CORBIS; 19 David Hosking/FLPA; 21 © Ashley Cooper/CORBIS

# Contents

Cockerel and hens

These chickens live together
on a farm.

Cockerel

tail feathers

comb

wattles

Chickens have pointed combs on their heads and flaps called wattles under their chins. Male cockerels have long tail feathers. The female hens are much smaller.

How many chickens can you see?

Hens

5

A nest for eggs

A hen makes a nest of straw. She lays one egg there every day. When she has mated with a cockerel, her eggs can grow into chickens.

Eggs are oval so that they roll in a circle and not out of the nest.

The hen sits on her eggs. The heat
of her body keeps them warm.
She turns the eggs every day
to keep them warm all over.

Inside an egg

A chick grows inside each egg. It grows bigger every day. Air and food travel along the red tubes in the egg to help the chick grow.

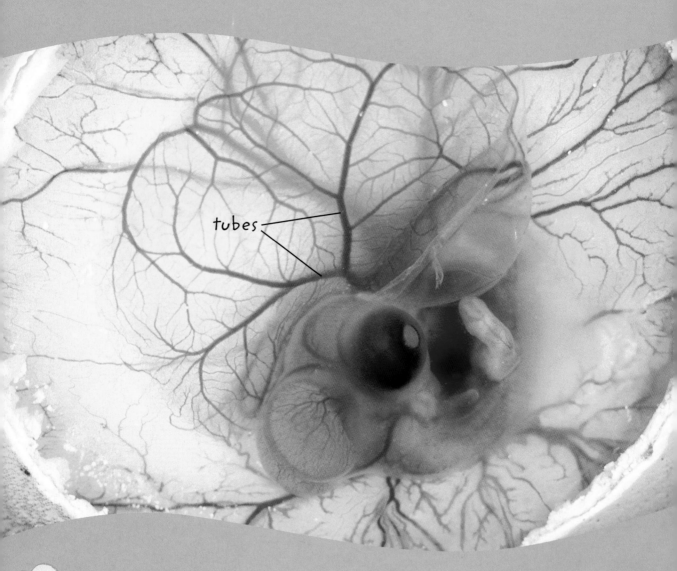

tubes

After three weeks, the chick
completely fills the egg. It is ready
to hatch.

Can you see the chick's eye, beak and foot?

Time to hatch

The chick has a sharp egg-tooth
on its beak. It taps
the eggshell
and makes
a hole in it.

It taps and taps
until the eggshell
cracks open.

Finally, the eggshell breaks apart
and the tiny chick hatches.
A new-born chick is damp
and sticky.

The chick is very tired after it has hatched. It rests for a while.

Fluffy chicks

Soon the chick can stand up and walk.
It shakes dry its soft, fluffy down.

This chick could fit inside your hand.

1 hour

Soon all the chicks have hatched.
The little chicks stay close together.
If they cannot see their mother,
they cheep loudly.

Chicks grip on
to a perch with
their curved toes
and claws.

Mother hen

The chicks follow their mother.
She shows them how to search
the ground for worms, insects
and seeds.

2 days

The chicks peck the food their mother
pecks and learn what is good to eat.

The hen covers the chicks with her wings to keep them warm and safe.

Growing feathers

Week by week the chicks
grow bigger and stronger.
Feathers grow on
their wings.

1 week

2 weeks

16

Soon the chicks have
feathers all over. Their comb
begins to grow, as well.

4
weeks

Chickens

By five months, the chickens are grown up. They look for their own food. At night, they roost in a hen house.

The chickens have grown a comb and wattles.

This chicken is digging a hole
in soft earth. It rolls around and
flaps its wings to clean its feathers.
This is called a dustbath.

Chickens
pull their feathers
with their beak to
keep them smooth.
This is called
preening.

19

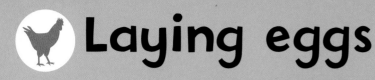

Laying eggs

The young hens are ready to lay eggs.
Some farmers take away hens' eggs
to sell for people to eat.

Egg-laying hens may lay up
to 300 eggs in their first year.

A farmer has let this hen keep her
eggs. These will soon turn into chicks.

Chicken life cycle

A hen lays eggs. When a hen and cockerel have mated, a chick grows inside an egg. The chicks hatch. After 5 months they become chickens.

eggs
Chickens lay eggs
in a nest.

hatching
The tiny chick breaks the
eggshell and hatches.

hen and cockerel
By 5 months, the chickens
are grown up.

chick
The chick grows bigger
and stronger.

Make a pop-up egg

Make a decorated egg and chick.

You will need:
- white card
- pencil • scissors
- felt-tip pens
- paper fastener

1. Draw an egg on white card. Cut it out and colour it.

2. Cut the egg in half with zig-zags.

3. Overlap the egg halves so that only the bottom zig zags show. Draw around this egg on to white card. Cut it out.

4. Draw a chick on the white egg and colour it.

5. Put the coloured egg on top of the white one. Push a paper fastener through the left-hand side of both eggs, where the zig-zags overlap. Open out the paper fastener.

23

Glossary

beak the hard pointed bit of a bird's mouth that it uses to pick up food

comb the red part that sticks up on the top of a chicken's head

down the first, light soft feathers that a chick is born with

female a girl chicken

hatch to break out of an egg

male a boy chicken

mate when a male and female come together so they can produce young

roost to sleep or sit at night

wattles the two red flaps under a chicken's chin

Index